THE
CELERY
FOREST

THE CELERY FOREST

Catherine Graham

POEMS

A Buckrider Book

Buckrider Books is an imprint of Wolsak and Wynn Publishers.

Cover image: *With an Owl in a Celery Forest* by Cora Brittan
Cover and interior design: Natalie Olsen, Kisscut Design
Author photograph: Portrait Boutique
Typeset in Fairfield
Printed by Coach House Printing Company Toronto, Canada

Canada Council   Conseil des Arts
for the Arts   du Canada

Canadian   Patrimoine
Heritage   canadien

ONTARIO ARTS COUNCIL
CONSEIL DES ARTS DE L'ONTARIO
an Ontario government agency
un organisme du gouvernement de l'Ontario

The publisher gratefully acknowledges the support of the Canada Council for the Arts, the Ontario Arts Council and the Government of Canada.

Buckrider Books
280 James Street North
Hamilton, Ontario
Canada L8R 2L3

Library and Archives Canada Cataloguing in Publication
Graham, Catherine, author
The celery forest / Catherine Graham.
Poems.
ISBN 978-1-928088-41-7 (softcover)
I. Title.
PS8563.R31452C45 2017   C811'.6   C2017-904884-8

FOR ANYONE WHOSE LIFE HAS
BEEN TOUCHED BY CANCER

Would you tell me, please,
which way I ought to go from here?

LEWIS CARROLL

Alice in Wonderland

Though you have the will of the wild birds

W.B. YEATS

"He Wishes His Beloved Were Dead"

Contents

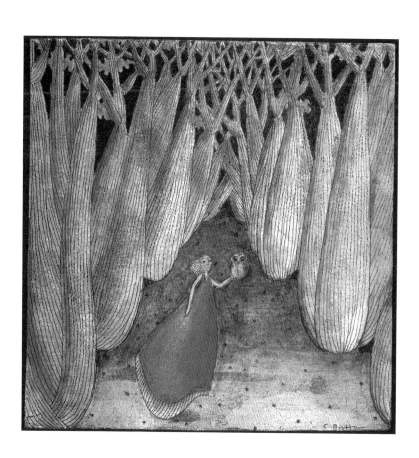

Interrogation in the Celery Forest

We shoulder it onto the slab.
It squirms. Water. Electric-white.

Raindrops fast into absence.
No bridge as believable as all this.

Pliers were used. And absence.
A heart – skewered through skeins

of red nets and milk from some aimless
animal on the drowning cloth.

Now, intruder, bird's-eye, pip,
you must answer.

Sheet Lightning Isn't Real Lightning, It's Just Far Away

He sits in the balcony of the screened-in porch
absorbing night. The arc of his chair

curves into radio-quiet. Called to her father's lap,
the young one sits. How will she recall

the X-ray of the dark when the small
world lit – green-fiery leaves about to burst,

rows of houses shining like clocks –
sun gone to the backlit side of a cloud.

What Birds They Were

They arrive, a cloud with wings and a brain –
they soar and hover, land on the celery trees.

They cloak the leaves. Black fruit, seed eyes.
They become what they are –

human-watchers, staring at the frozen girl
strewn on the lawn. They drop

her temperature. She feels snow, her blue
lungs. Her mind floats – pastel clouds,

a glint of buckle, high and dry in the bird-free air –
she coils lightning into the double helix of herself.

Pact

I stole money to buy birds.
Planted them in the sky
past the concrete fields –

I heard them singing
to the dirt, clear as any tune
lodged in the Celery Forest.

Flightmaps

Outside birds play house:
find the right mate; find

the right tree. Flightmaps
in air, the traffic of matter.

There before
and there thereafter

they've stolen the hum
from a mother's mouth.

A coin falls into a piggy bank
and a girl draws flowers

with a green pen.
A father, home

from work, places
comics on her desk.

Richie Rich, Archie,
Casper the Friendly Ghost. She hears

the revving silence
of the Singer.

Zipper

The fat tongue on his T-shirt
eager for flavour, and beneath it, the growing
pink he'd unzipped – no adults to tug

us back except this twist in the blood –
run! The mud soft-shucking our shoes –
don't look, don't fall –

she screamed between our broken breath –
you asked, you touched! – fast
inside her cousin's house

while I stood chained to the sound
of the lock sliding time forward
and back into place like a zipper.

Senior Class Trip

Her glazed eyes open to the hotel dark.
Watch it work through her sleep.
She bolts upright, mewling. The sight
she sees is not for us. Three roommates.

How well does one know the other?
Her white-clenched bedsheets are knuckled
tight. Caged, she spits gibberish in fast
random, a Zeppelin record playing

backwards and all those touches
pulsing from within, indenting from
a core so deep, whitewashing her face –
stop stop stop – she shoves the vastness off –

it comes back. We hear the grunt.
We stand watching what happened happen
while below us the slaughter of New York
sirens are approaching some other terror.

American Woodcock

Intruder among daffodils, tulips,
cryptic in the mean
neighbour's garden, you sat

planted as a dare with your narrow
bill of pale brown tipped
like a dipping bird into a glass beaker

without the force for swinging back.
We wanted to jab you with our sticks,
make you twitch – *bird puppet!* –

avoid your poker beak;
cage you in a mist net. You just
sat there, caught in our own trap

of indecision, until your short wings
flipped air into flight –
leaving us wild for your name.

Red-eyed Vireo

You are difficult to find
among summer leaves, though I hear your song.

I place a pillow under my shoulder,
my arm behind my head.

Slowly, methodically, you scan the canopy for caterpillar prey,
I still can't see you.

I move the pads of my fingers
around my left breast.

From early morning to late evening, your incessant song,
the same question and answer.

I use light, medium and firm
pressure. Still, you're there.

Waiting for the Diagnosis

If we weren't holding hands, it wasn't
from fighting. No portent
on leaves, not yet. Only the Haliburton

Forest, full of birth – the Eden
we crave during winter's run. Then came
the scream. An animal – somewhere –

inside another animal's throat, followed
by that cold, testing silence we wore
as shivers, as scales, down our back.

Cancer in the Celery Forest

Who knew the celery could branch so high?
Each stalk finger-stiff, each canopy
an open umbrella.

A girl in red holds an owl,
perched on her hand
like a concrete thought.

There is wisdom within
the Celery Forest –
all the dropped stars have faces.

The Royal Mole Catcher

Come up, I'll be your wild cat,
weasel – you,
who pockmark the great

Gardens of Versailles
by running riot underground, clever,
slippery as buried water.

Prongs of steel smash
to the bone –
it killed a Bourbon king.

Myopic and nearly deaf, tossing
dirt with those giant paws –
I hear each snap in my sleep.

The Pigeon Fancier

To fly them farther, faster, proves your bloodline's
tough. Sure, I embrace the widowhood system –
hens pre-race – they fuel the cocks.

I start them young. Month old, a few kilometres.
Then I tenderly edge them to over one hundred.
Not all come back – power line, Cooper's hawk.

Mink! Little shit tore a hole through the mesh.
Killed half. Left me with stiff,
bloodied birds. It couldn't eat thirty.

So, you start again. Breed a better bloodline.
Eliminate the weak, sickly, over-the-hill,
anticipate the heat from the flight on your hands.

Wave

Gulls with names I do not know, brooding.
Their metallic cries wreck the wind's talk.

The patina, the pop, like oil in a pan. Like heat
that isn't there. What else eludes us?

The Pacific unpacks its weight, packs,
unpacks again. The tease of whitecapped surf.

When whole, we ride the world beneath a wave,
each little animal, tough inside us, attuned to the crash.

Lake

You, dark waters, skimming the surface
of pebbles, the effect is breath,
not dark, you and your sand-wash
into thoughts of white, curling the rim,
your seeping stretches around smaller islands
and shores of crab boats landing north.

And so it goes. Again meets again –

Violets

She spoke violets, the stems' stretch,
water drying out, piano lid, a teasing mouth.

She made her daughter ache for sound, for more
than air moving through the nostrils, mouth.

Mother, speak!
When her long, grey hair uncoiled, the clicks

of metal hairpins settled decades later
in her granddaughter's night-grinding teeth.

Deciduous

Leaves dry out, become castanets, shaking.
Quiver. Tethered birds until one whispers – *Go!*
A sheet of starlings falls, winter's push.

Leaves curl, hands reach up –
take me back. No longer hidden,
abandoned nests in plain sight.

I see them everywhere after the diagnosis.
Black knots in X-rays – first
discovered by a circling hand.

They stay high in the air, waiting
for breasts that never come back.

The Fawn

Why the fawn with the missing foot?
She circles within the Celery Forest

as if it were a cage. She invites me in.
Her neck has thinned from my small hands

wringing the cotton silk. Her missing foot –
it shows me where the rain fits.

Beside the White Chickens

I have released the white chickens.
They are roaming on the moon.

They flurry past large doorways –
a release of matryoshka dolls

holding chickens within chickens,
waiting to be hatched –

to extend the red feeling,
to retract the red feeling.

Migration

She holds birds in her bones,
air of bone. Flight path
wind-designed.

Uprooted, she walks, turns
into forest. Birds fly through her –
a cemetery of leaves.

Undergrowth

The pea beneath
your mattress
makes tornadoes.

Your pale feet
grow rubies,
and the rotating wind

is a mother's eye.
What hovers?
The technician

with the needle
as she guns her target.
Ka-chaw ka-chaw ka-chaw –

a crow with no body
under its smooth,
black feathers.

MRI

No metal implants or fragments.

A long, fibrous stalk.

You signed consent, removed jewellery.

Face down through the doughnut hole.

Tapering into leaves.

Contrast material running through your veins.

Magnets. Pinnate to bipinnate with rhombic leaflets.

Still – lie still.

You've been given earphones, a padded table.

Seeds are broad ovoids.

Cushioned openings for breasts to hang.

Grown in an open garden.

Thumping. Clicking. Knocks and taps.

The celery's a cleansing tonic.

Whirs with car-accident screeches –

a father's skull, mother's mouth.

Wide range of cultivars.

The technician stands in a nearby room.

Inside, a seed; inside, a small fruit.

The Littlest Thing Missed

Inside my hands are the roots
of hers: tendrils, fingers.

Smallest shell of matryoshka dolls
before the others enclose, expand.

Owl in the Celery Forest

Owl, you never asked to be wise
or a companion to the witch.

Fly in for the scurry – vole, field mouse,
creatures with eyes scuttling through grass.

Then pluck the tumour out of my breast
with your sharp, curved talons –

let the only thing that spreads be your wings.

She Sounds Almost Human

Vowels, consonants, diphthongs, syllables
reconstructed into something robotic-like.
This. Hello. Hat. Honey. Fool.
Anonymity is no worry. Our "she" is
formed from studio erosion, the con-
catenation becoming voice of our
generation. The ocean pleasures
of wheat-blowing grass is not the solution
behind artificial sound-quest for
perfection. *Oracle. Ogre.* Harmony
is only a hair's breadth away from real
life. Her voice lowers. Your attention
drops. Time is clay. Who will predict the
conclusion between the mechanics of her lips
and the tragedy of forked lightning,
the electric sound-cloud in a cup?

Cloud In Situ

When we look up, shapes we've never seen before
hanging from a bone of cloud, countless udders
holding viewers captive.

In situ: in its place.
Like manners – please stay in,
thank you for listening.

The weather warned us –
climactic sky of fungus-green
against chalk-black.

Hightailing pilot, newly licensed,
and I, your eager passenger. We enter
blue that can't be seen once inside it.

Lost, we land on a cirrus cloud. I walk out. *See?*
Clouds are solid. Drops of water, tight as ice.
You worry for my return.

I Dream I Leave the Quarry Again

I don't know how, but again I own it –
the land-surround of water and stone.
Hub of blue or ice basin, always
fish-heavy. The drowned down there,
machinery, plush with algae.
(Having long made the man-made: *Mine!*)
A room to dive into or skate shakily
across. An eye of moist or a tight-lipped
mouth. Weather sensitive, the wait
for air to take lead: whitecap rough
or opal smooth. Tree-cloud illusion –
a mirror you walk on – to sink, to be
immersed – *hold your dreaming breath,*
then come back up. Come up.

The Sparrow That Isn't There

A woman's shoe is the movement of a bird
in my peripheral vision. The hopping

lilt of a sentence with teeth lifting
from the tongue. It's almost spring, almost, and

the long, trembling snowfall is madly human,
and the sparrow, a catastrophe, frozen, and not there.

Winterhill

The heat glossing their backs. Moon licking the river

white. They thrive at night. Born nocturnal,
they smell the rub of dew slipping out.

To see through darkness blocked by moon, cloud, star.
Where is the water? The bullfrog knows.

The spring peeper. Their growing chorus itches the air.
There is no gate to pass. Just a metallic scent

they cannot detect. What hits, kills. Curled
into carcass, rot, on beds of gravel and dirt, they lie

ready to receive a birth of fly and maggot. But the lifting
fog is a trail becoming from the non-soul's heat, the organs' stop.

All instinct from inside them now furring air with whitish vale, shadow's
trick of weight. Here is where the dead live on – ghost animals –

in a world called Winterhill. They've become a floating pond,
a threshold of in-between, moist portal where water

finds water and fixes to air – *there, there.*

Beady Teardrops Lead to Trees

Black stores of infinitesimal cyanide, beady teardrops
lead to trees – roots, rings, branches, *fruit*.

There. I said that word. Now screw the crisp
sour it holds; the mangy pulp inside the light-sucked sheen.

Sun-round on its stem, keep it hanging there
before my stomach curdles up the whole stinking pink mass.

I am no Eve. Even the hidden seeds mean me. In time
I seed a deepening wisdom as the vial inside me implodes.

Constant Stranger

Swallow me, Celery Forest.
Your chewing erases calories.
Plus times minus. Small

becomes large in your ripeness,
where rabbits splice the borders, wild
cells never cease. The dead

keep asking: *what time do we have here?*
Footfalls land between the constant
stranger, the patient self.

When I Think of Your Aging Mouth

If my prone body had become the top layer
of sedimentary rock, I'd feel the sun's heat,

not coldness in a box. Twenty
mattresses stacked beneath me. The ceiling,

a kiss away; stipples of topographical maps
with the world turned upside down.

When I think of your aging mouth –
only sound waves, I tell myself. But the gasp inside me

grows, a seed splits through the first of twenty mattresses
and weeds of hot air flower from my mouth.

Fire Glass

Blame it on the screw
tightening the slack waist
of an hourglass.

Touch, a measure of heat.
Freckle, the end
of a match.

We rolled in smoke
despite the fire glass,
torn cloud with no address while

far beneath –
an animal trapped –

cries through hotel walls –
grasses of hair pushing through –

The Day in January Most People Die at Their Own Hands

You can't just say anything.
The moon's white lie

shudders the water
and makes a black pathway

of eider ducks gloss
against the white.

It's the glisten we're after
before the after comes.

I Am One of 1,511 Patients Resting at Lakeshore Psychiatric Hospital Cemetery

My life is more important than my ghost.
The truth – orphan, spinster, Cottage D.
Floating through brick and other strange
appearances. A strangled curtain, light's trick.
It's cold being dead, being atoms in all
elements. Rumours of babies, fetus-deep
beneath the old working orchard means
apples and pears have faces. *Busiest
haunt in the city.* Patients and staff
never reported sightings. A ghost
is a fold in a slip of mind, frantic
nut of contagion. That fly at your neck.

Glass Animals

Their loud roar
resides in my room

where silence breeds
bars and gates.

Air can't split them open.
Glass animals know this.

The Uncanny Valley

And when we die, we fall into the trough of the uncanny valley.
— MASAHIRO MORI, "The Uncanny Valley"

Never born into our own.
We are the unborn; slipping

in, we nest inside, carry
languages we don't know.

Toys. Dolls. Stuffed animals.
We move through children's hands.

Our season is new. No time to flower.
Lifeless, we watch you grow

cold – your colour changes,
your movement ceases –

into the uncanny valley
where you fall below us.

The Rose Census

A romantic seeks out the Adam garden.
Slips over the locked gate –
trellis after trellis in a bee-drunken state –

the boozing of roses, the shot glass of roses.
These are the shades that torch skin.
When he reaches one hundred –

that's the end for the body the rose-counter
resides in. No diagnosis.
Skull into soil, bones, corrosion.

Orchid Painting, Room 19

Stare and they multiply.
Beads on bloom-red.
Yellow rust between pink petals
seed inside the paint.

Stare and they multiply.
To count is to lose count.
Beads, dots, circles –
call them anything but cells.

Masks

I entered Chaos through the plastic mask
of anaesthesia. Styx to bones that don't break,
just the lessening landscape beside a nipple
that never milked yet puckers pink. I need

a deeper slit on the left to secure clean margins
plus a sentinel undercut – Hospital déjà vu,
a dawn re-entering as Sun dreams. No nail polish
on hands. Baby-naked beneath a stiff blue gown

falling open at the front without a pre-op grip.
How summer dissolves spring and autumn into masks
that seasons make from spin and tilt. I am made

more uneven above the heart. *Wake up!*
Maternal presence never felt since her Christmas
death. The age she died hiding inside me.

It Begins When You're Not Looking, Stops When You Are

My Kool-Aid is dripping, tomato soup's overcooked, clams with red sauce, leak week, Li'l Red, my little friend, joining the cast of *Pad Men*, on the blob, Crayola red, ninja red, Uncle Red, code red, Satan's baby, birthing a blood diamond, opening the floodgates, I'm having the painters in, surfing the crimson, riding the cotton pony, Carrie at the prom, rusty pipes, Miss Scarlett has returned to Tara, shark week, the Great Flood cometh, on the rag, the visitor, juice press, moon time, red wedding, on Wednesdays we wear pink, my bloody valentine, lining the drawers, Aunt Ruby is visiting, having a party at my pad, the Red Baron, experiencing technical difficulties, dredging the love canal, the server is down, the kitty is sick, expelling my hysteria, flying my colours, lady days, Mother Nature, T.O.M., ragging, "the regular discharge of blood and mucosal tissue from the inner lining of the uterus through the vagina" – air – air – end of sentence.

Loggerhead

Dive from an elevated pitch, sit and wait,
you black-masked hunter in service

of the hooked beak. Small. No talons.
Compensate. Sever the neck of small invertebrates.

Spike onto sharp projections. Impale and anchor
on a barbed-wire fence. Thorns are stakes.

Left to ripen – amphibian, lizard, rodent –
a red-housed ladybug, a nine-eyed stare.

Shrike

Now come songbirds with hooked
beaks, eager for discarded body parts
trashed in plastic, coddled in blood.

With a feather-white apron down
their necks, masked with slashes
of night, they scoop, fly and fix

their finds on hawthorn branches.
Impaled, our tumours hang –
liver, pancreas, uterus, earlobe, breast –

thorns are for tearing off.
Tree in bloom. Sweet, savage
butcher bird, devour our cancers. Thrive.

Notes from the Celery Forest

They snap when pulled apart. Tight, compact,
without stalks that splay, leaves
pale to bright green when free from yellow patches.

Cut into pieces of desired length, remove
fibrous strips by peeling Myrmidon horses
that once grazed wild celery fields.

Céleri, seleri, serino – blackheart
not caused by insects. They arc the cave of Calypso.
Chthonian symbol among Ancient Greeks.
They emerged from the blood of Kadmilos.

Spicy odours from dark, leafy colours
led to the cult of death. But flowers remain
creamy white, dense compound umbels.
And the round stem is more bitter in flavour.

Red Rain of Kerala

They said it could, it couldn't happen.
It came, they said, post–sonic boom,
post–crash of light, the raining red
that they said lasted till it stopped.
The beads of blood that wet the earth
returned as water to the world.
They said it was mammalian blood. A flood
of bats met meteorite. They called them spores,
red algae spores, red fly ash, red clay, fungus rust.

Breakwater

Pipe-staked, dynamite-stuffed limestone, blasted slabs
of fossil rock, time-press of ancient seas, sediments
snail into shellish shapes, creature tracks like hieroglyphics,
the cut rock – scooped and horse-carted out –
slowly, the hole fills ... and up like an escaping creature,

a liquid cemetery air sac for abandoned machinery.
Hoofprints, bootprints dissolve to fish
inside the growing fluid. Water, now free to roam, softens
walls of its open-air cage, whitecapped, flat, cottonseed-coated,
leafed, sun-loved or winter-taken, the wait for forms to crawl out.

Sunrise with Sea Monsters

after J. M. W. Turner

Wide awake like a parent or spouse,
the worry, having inched
down my spine, crawls
into my mouth: where were you?

    The sun rallies against this.
    Monsters make more from too many.

He stands at the front door,
a Breathalyzer sticker on his chest.
Floating letters gleam
He did not pass.

    There is only so much light to make sea.
    To keep crew tasked to unfinished business.

Downcast, he stares at my fingers,
waiting for the wag and point.
Relief. My father's alive.
I shut my eyes to keep from waking up.

    Mine is a false cry behind scurvy clouds,
    where all the fevered brushstrokes have drowned.

The Mine Pattern

Shade interest with a harvest, a rare limbo triggers no claim.
Feather, shaft, rachis. Who hears inside a scream? Voices
move through hands, another score for silence. Silver-haired

disturbance as old as a bat. Let sleep be easy.
You unfold to me, my long-dead mother, the loss
between rare and sake. Understorey is overstorey despite the
    mine pattern.

Recall the loneliness of snails.
The colour figure is disappearing.
You lose less when you're most like yourself.

Water lilies, masks for illness. Fall open blue gown.
The feather is quite intricate on fabric: barb, barbule, hook
    and latch.
Some lose all feathers at once. *I have a gecko I talk to in
    North Carolina.*

Who can grasp meaning in that? The spot on the screen
darts in and out, squamous and flat. A bird's
survival depends on the condition of its feathers.

Fireflies

Little green fires that do not burn,
yet blink and float
outside the cottage window
stringing night
into Christmas trees.
When you returned
as a firefly, I heard
what happened –
your winking battery
broken because you merely
grew in size.
Jealous of Dad's sighting,
not knowing you would appear
decades later as pure
waves the moment I broke
free from anaesthesia's grip.

My Father Was a Bird

Freewheeling dove, sparrow, starling,
never of the flock, his quills
beneath his skin, his wing tattoo
prepared him, stamped predestination,
he practised flight with each flex of his bicep –
to be sky-borne for six seconds –
his flight through the flying car.

Vociferous

I have circled this image before.
The deer on the road, the dark, the car

belonging to my father. Taken
in by your call when you fly-spiral

the train tracks on my way home from school.
Burnt screech and a broken wing. Too close

to the nest; what I couldn't see
as you trailed false pain – a loose

page from an over-loved book, so ready
to be airborne as pure wing.

Passing over the railway tracks to head
downhill, I left you healing your ruse injury;

your call inside me: *kill-deer kill-deer kill-deer*

They Will Take My Island

after Arshile Gorky

Scuttle in the blood cells, they seed
the white beach, crawl sideways
under the skin with a belly-skeletal undertaking.

Pincer-caught without pain, they labour
up a rogue wave of metastasis
to make the spreading endless.

Siren

I lure them to me with the milky
notes from my chest. Fools
will say suicide, unaware
of the sequins, the scales binding

ankles, knees and thighs, ending
two fingers below the pearl
of my navel. Freed
in new constraint, I swim –

sheathed by fish, their eyes vacant
as air bubbles. No void
for men to mine, to grunt
out their sex. They drown for me.

Egret

To see underwater. To see
through skin. To stab

at what moves is to reveal
your beak, the scissor, the incision

of scale to flesh. O vulnerable
heartbeat from being cut open –

no jacket to zip – just a steady
stitching beneath the whir

of mother's Singer from the drugged
language of my brain where the lawn

between the egret's pinhole eyes
becomes the grass I once walked on.

Scar

no barbs
or barbules
just shaft

what fell from sky
split me open
now sealed ceiling-tight

the rachis fading
on my chest

a feather
has as much air
as matter

Colony

At what point does the ice-free plain,
wind-flattened, cold, home
to a colony of gentoo penguins,

make one juvenile fledge
past its nest of pebbled edges
to see his neighbours close-up.

A thrill for little wanderer.
Over there is here.
Eyes stare. Bodies move in, closer.

The first peck suggests *storm,*
consequence the next, the next –
the air is packed with pecking.

The Day She Celebrated Most

In a clinical room, pain is a state
of mind, a pincushion for punctures.

Season of boughs and berries,
built from the busy network

of her hands. Insistence
from a sentence wanting otherwise.

The crystal beads she glued to plastic fruit –
pears and apples she then twist-tied

to the Christmas tree – spread on clothes.
Found, months later, gems of cut light.

Sheet Music for Breathing in the Radiation Room

after John Cage

Ratchet silence, I hear ammunition hammer.
Go on, health is a backwards trip. Yelps

before baby steps, tantrums, kicking candy
in the hourglass. Hex and melt each fixin'.

Toss the mulch of *yes*. Hush and play 4'33"
under the spell she was. Don't melt. Don't.

Question the tunnel. Horse-throw black cattle.
Terraform black suns of stemmed plucked flowers.

Let mother's hands play trickster the bird before
a plenary nap. Let scorched petals fall at your feet.

After Radiation

The Russian doll was taken out –
babies, babies, eons ago, cracked
dry from petrified lava. O volcano,

no head of Orpheus with vowels
to sponge the language. To be left alone
is to be found patient for surgical weather.

.

A Leash of Deer

Untamable creatures, spotted as trout lily, camouflaged umber,
tawny, branched with satellite ears, air-cupped to the heartbeat
   of the ground.

Extended line between sun-dawn moon-dusk – a leash of deer.
Which site brought forth the first? Allowed leggy form to lift

up and off the forest floor into white-tailed leaps, or red, or roe.
No matter. Kill. Suffocation. Quick throat-slit. Kill and stop
   the leash of deer

from spreading out so when that fall night rears, a father driving
   home, one road
away from home, no cloven-hoofed ungulate on Stonemill Road,
   parting from a field

of parting corn, from stalk and husk and rustle beside a frog-thick
   croaking ditch, to trigger
panic – the swerve – a father would have made it back to bed,
   exhaling O's of alcohol through

greying shades of stubble, and a daughter would awaken to the
   muffle of his morning
snores through cedar walls and not the 3 a.m. knocking at her
   bedroom door, the waiting cop.

The Trick of Seeing Stars

The air between each bird is a flock
of anti-feathers, part of the migration, flow
of rolling air they navigate as water.

It's land that gives them trouble.
The full moon disappears. One thousand miles
and more. To be at ease in water, what grebes do.

A water bird is never wet. Their wings tire.
The full moon disappears. They view the dark
by city lights; it's like the trick of seeing stars.

Look up, you'll see each elongated body, neck
shaped into a boat, oncoming fleet. Smear
of city lights, the birds see water there, a temporary

stop en route to Mexico. Downing by instinct,
they extend their far-back feet and hit
the car-dark pavement – water birds are never wet.

Tell Us Where the Dead Go

All the recent ghosts
harbour water veils.

Fog seeds. Wet drapery for fruit,
skinless as our fear of the invisible.

Clear as soul
in a cage called skin.

To think we won't rise
as water proves we're fools.

What the Dying Don't Say

Through whorls of drugged ears, warblers, thrushes,
notes reverberate down our throats where

clavicles shift, no, whole shoulders, twin avian blades –
we fly cold to the ceiling and stare down from the moon.

The Hard Sweep

I bring his broom inside me. The one he used
to sweep clumps of cottonwood-fluff

off window screens; sticky as adhesives
over wounds. It blocked his view to the quarry.

It wanted his world to grow white, to match
the state of his heart. Attached to his broom,

his long arm of determination, reach –
I hear his mourning scrapes inside the left

side of my chest, the hard sweep to remove cells
survivors fear most. His unstoppable chore has come.

Oak

If a lidded box doesn't announce *death*

a headstone will. Granite each visit.
Never bones, bones appearing as roots.
Just brush of wind, sun on hand.

Leave stone for flower.

But she keeps coming back,
the casket won't close, a beckoning
hand with gnarled fingers – roots

from underground
refusing to go underground.

Talk to her. Tell her –

It's time. Stop haunting me. I can't sleep –

You dream of trees.

Self-Portrait in Clay

What made it a head – the softness of the clay, beads stuffed
in eye sockets. Curls through a sieve, like wonder thickening.
No sense in that. The kiln fires everything up.
Chemo playing invisible through the overburden of light.

Each Scaly God Ensconced in Sex

Winter hisses at the house. Edges. Slips
in like mice. Those moans are not you.

Months later, a silence breaks. Candling black. Crack
and fissure, melt soft along the edges, steal

blue from white and open
slowly – a thought bubbles out.

Rock-bottom, the fish unlock their winter weight.
They rise, breeding organs, ensconced in sex.

Littlefoot

after Ted Hughes

O littlefoot, through the dirt,
your green sac of seed, your c-cupped ribs, growing petioles.

O littlefoot, you keep to the pattern of green on green, push
open your umbrella with earth's slow consent.

O littlefoot, landscape for thrips and woolly aphids, you tease
rabbits' hunger, throw laughter 'round your fence.

My hands are blue. Bring the blood in close. Extremities are the first
to lose heat. Split me into strings, sing to my fears, O littlefoot.

Recurrence

Return to the Celery Forest. Accept the changes
in your sleep, unbroken dreams from the dead,

the built-in expiry date. When you are certain
the sofa's talking to the chair, hover –

Lily of the valley, a gladiola away from the catkin-drip sun
where air is birdsong and blue one rows across.

This hurts and it's meant to, the quiet of a final score.
Rain Brailles the window. I'll need a lifetime to read.

Acknowledgements

Versions of these poems have appeared in *Catherines, the Great* anthology (forthcoming), *Crannóg Magazine* (Ireland), *CV2, Eyewear* blog (UK), *The Fiddlehead, FreeFall* magazine, *Glasgow Review of Books, Grey Borders, Gutter Magazine* (Scotland), *The Humber Literary Review, Koffler Centre of the Arts* website, *LRC, GUSH: Menstrual Manifestos for Our Times* (forthcoming), *Minola Review, Room Magazine, The Rusty Toque, Southword Journal* (Ireland), *Sunrise with Sea Monsters* blog, *They Will Take My Island* blog, *The Ulster Tatler, What's Your Story? Anthology* and *White Wall Review.* My thanks to the editors.

The quote used at the end of "It Begins When You're Not Looking, Stops When You Are" comes from *Menstruation and the Menstrual Cycle Fact Sheet* (Washington, DC: Office on Women's Health, 2014), quoted in "Menstruation," *Wikipedia*, last modified July 22, 2017, https://en.wikipedia.org/wiki/Menstruation#cite_note-Women2014Men-2.

I am grateful to the following people for their valuable feedback and friendship: Merry Benezra, Ian Burgham, Dolores Hayden, Bruce Hunter, Jeanette Lynes, James Martin, Ruth Roach Pierson and Patrick Woodcock. Thanks to Ginger Pharand and her daughter, Angeline, for the text that inspired the poem "Winterhill" and to Madhur Anand, co-author of the research paper that inspired "The Mine Pattern" ("The Scientific Value of the Largest Remaining Old-growth Red Pine Forests in North America").

I'd also like to thank the wonderful and supportive team at Wolsak & Wynn: Noelle Allen, Ashley Hisson and Joe Stacey. Thanks to Emily Dockrill Jones for her copy-editing, Cora Brittan for the captivating mixed-media piece *With an Owl in a Celery Forest*, which graces the cover, and to Natalie Olsen for the book's stunning design. I am deeply grateful for the love and support of my life partner, John Coates. Lastly, I'd like to thank my dear editor, Paul Vermeersch, for his ongoing faith in my poetry and his exquisite editing.

Catherine Graham is the author of five acclaimed poetry collections, including *Her Red Hair Rises with the Wings of Insects*, which was a finalist for the Raymond Souster Award and the CAA Award for Poetry, and the debut novel *Quarry*. Winner of the International Festival of Authors' Poetry NOW competition, she teaches creative writing at the University of Toronto where she won an Excellence in Teaching Award and at Humber College's Creative Book Publishing Program. Published internationally, she lives in Toronto. Visit her website at www.catherinegraham.com. Follow her on Twitter and Instagram @catgrahampoet.